P9-DMH-474

Mealtime Blessings

Copyright © 1999 Publications International, Ltd.
All rights reserved. This publication may not be reproduced or quoted
in whole or in part by any means whatsoever without written permission from

Louis Weber, C.E.O.
Publications International, Ltd.
7373 North Cicero Avenue
Lincolnwood, Illinois 60646

Permission is never granted for commercial purposes.
Manufactured in China.

8 7 6 5 4 3 2 1

ISBN: 0-7853-3902-7

Mealtime Blessings

Adapted by Lynne Suesse

Cover illustrated by Judith Pfeiffer, Linda Prater

Interior illustrated by
Judith Pfeiffer, Tish Tenud, Jennifer Fitchwell

Publications International, Ltd.

Come, Lord Jesus,
Be our guest.
Let these gifts
To us be blessed.

God is great,
God is good,
And we thank Him
For our food.
Amen.

Let us in peace eat the food
that God has provided for us.
Praise be to God for all His gifts.
Amen.

Our Hands We Fold

Our hands we fold,
  Our heads we bow,
For food and drink
  We thank Thee now.

While they were eating
Jesus took bread,
gave thanks and broke it.

Matthew 26:26

It is very nice to think
The world is full
of meat and drink,
With little children
saying grace
In every Christian
kind of place.

Each time we eat,
may we remember
God's love.
Amen.

18

God, we thank You
  For this food,
For rest and home
  And all things good:
For wind and rain
  And sun above,
But most of all
  For those we love.

Maryleona Frost

Thank you, O Lord, for Thy gifts which we are about to receive from Thy bounty.

Amen.

Thank you for the world so sweet,
Thank you for the food we eat.
Thank you for the birds that sing,
Thank you, God, for everything.

For every cup and plateful,
God, make us truly grateful!

Amen.